Especially Popular Christmas

7 Christmas Favorites Arranged for Late Intermediate Pianists

Dennis Alexander

As a child, I remember listening to Elvis Presley's "Blue Christmas" on my parent's big Curtis Mathes record player/TV console, which, at the time, I thought was almost the "coolest" thing I had ever heard. What fun it has been to take some of my personal favorite "pop" Christmas songs and arrange them for various levels! So many of these titles are timeless and remain popular with people of all ages. In *Especially Popular Christmas, Book 3,* enjoy a touching "Believe" from the movie *The Polar Express,* a quiet and tender "Blue Christmas," the beloved Jim Brickman song "The Gift," as well as many other arrangements that, when shared with others, are sure to elicit a smile along with a touch of nostalgia. Enjoy the holidays, and may you "Have Yourself a Merry Little Christmas!"

Blessings,

Produced by
Alfred Music Publishing Co., Inc.
P.O. Box 10003
Van Nuys, CA 91410-0003
alfred.com

Printed in USA.

ISBN-10: 0-7390-7359-1
ISBN-13: 978-0-7390-7359-9

Cover photo: © istockphoto / VisualField

Believe
(from *The Polar Express*)

Words and Music by
Alan Silvestri and Glenn Ballard
Arr. by Dennis Alexander

Gently and flowing

4

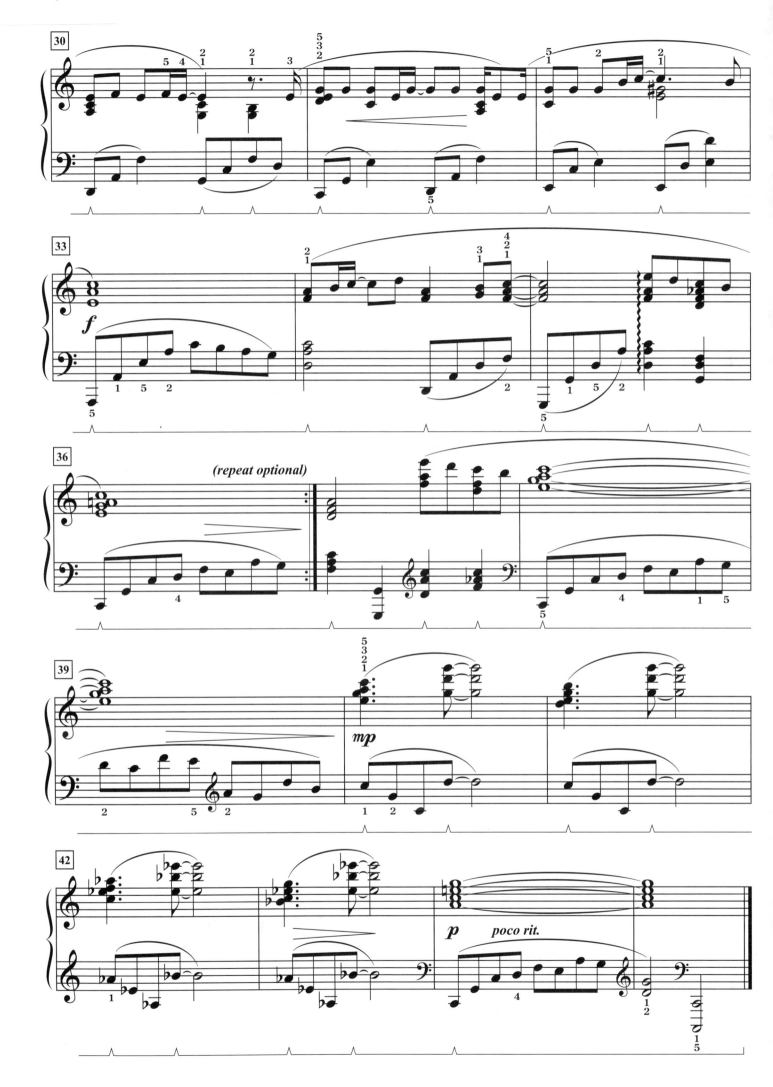

Blue Christmas

Words and Music by
Bill Hayes and Jay Johnson
Arr. by Dennis Alexander

O Holy Night (Cantique de Noel)

By Adolph Adam
Arr. by Dennis Alexander

9

Mistletoe and Holly

Words and Music by
Frank Sinatra, Dok Stanford and Henry Sanicola
Arr. by Dennis Alexander

(There's No Place Like)
Home for the Holidays

Words by Al Stillman
Music by Robert Allen
Arr. by Dennis Alexander

Winter Wonderland

Words by Dick Smith
Music by Felix Bernard
Arr. by Dennis Alexander

The Gift

Words and Music by
Jim Brickman and Tom Douglas
Arr. by Dennis Alexander

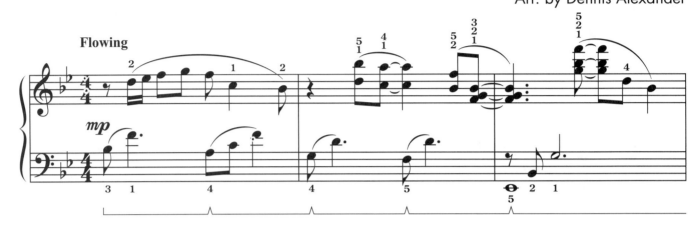

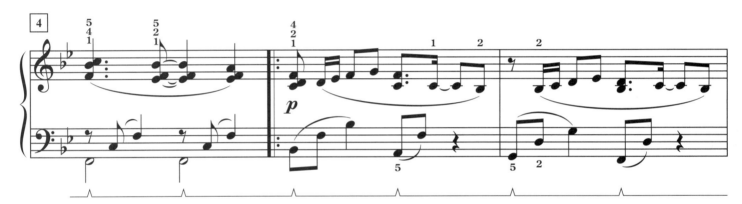

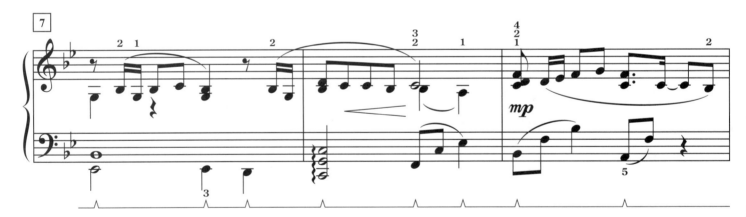

24

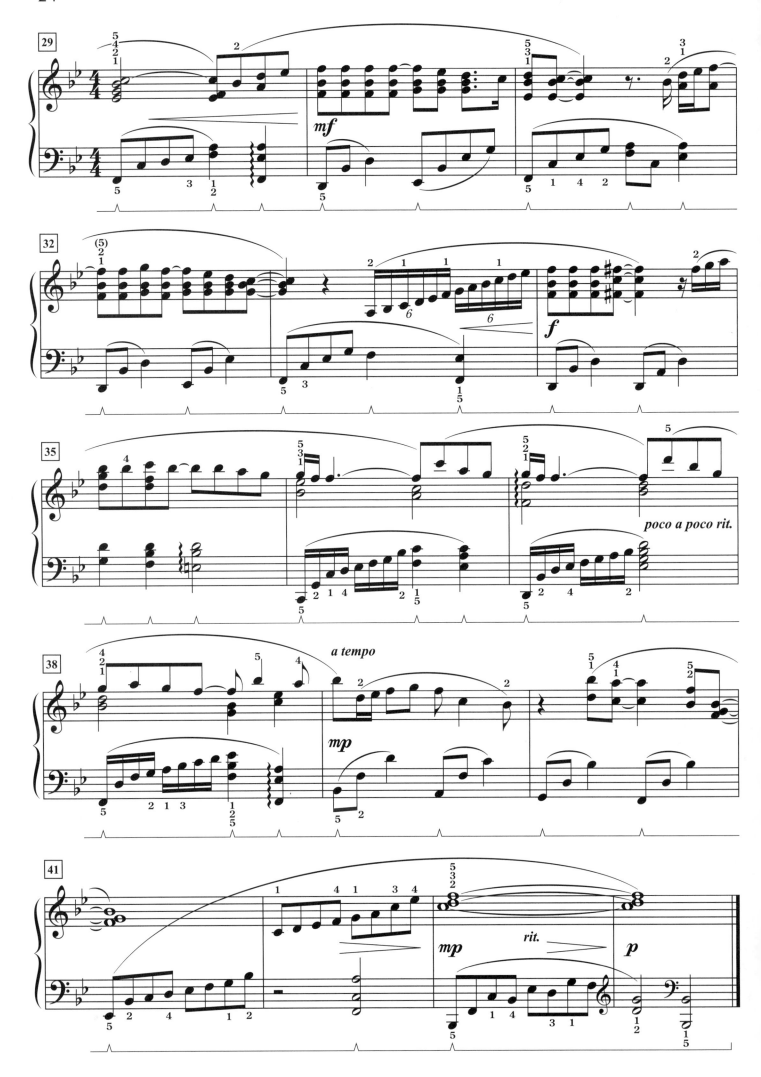

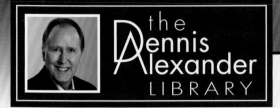

the Dennis Alexander LIBRARY

SOLO COLLECTIONS

Animal Magic (11730) E
Best of Dennis Alexander, The
  Book 1 (14693) E–LE
  Book 2 (14694) EI–I
Christmas Fantasy, A (6559) LI–EA
Christmas Silhouettes (6006) I
Christmas Splendor (16918) I–LI
Christmas Tree-O!, A (for 1, 2, or 3 players)
  Book (14515) LE
  GM Disk (14516)
Dennis Alexander's Favorite Solos
  Book 1 (24601) E–LE
  Book 2 (24602) EI–I
  Book 3 (24603) LI–EA
Especially for Adults
  Book 1 (27766) EI–I
  Book 2 (27767) I
  Book 3 (28233) LI
Especially for Boys (18868) LE
Especially for Christmas
  Book 1 (31387) EI–I
  Book 2 (31388) I
  Book 3 (31389) LI
Especially for Girls (18867) LE
Finger Paintings
  Book 1 (16815) EE
  Book 2 (17197) E
  Book 3 (17205) LE
Folk Song Silhouettes (6013) I
Jazz SophistiCAT (Alexander/Thurmond)
  Solo Book 1 (14715) LE–EI
  Solo Book 2 (14716) I
  Solo GM Disk 1 (14406)
  Solo GM Disk 2 (14407)
Just for You
  Book 1 (405) E
  GM Disk Book 1 (14437)
  Book 2 (406) LE–EI
  GM Disk Book 2 (14438)
  Book 3 (407) EI–I
  GM Disk Book 3 (14439)
  CD for Books 1–3 (16457)
  Book 4 (22484) I–LI
Keys to Artistic Performance
(Alexander/Clarfield)
  Book 1 (29991) EI–I
  Book 2 (29992) I–LI
Keys to Stylistic Mastery
  Book 1 (21363) LE–EI
  Book 2 (21364) EI–I
  Book 3 (22447) I–LI
Magic of Music, The
  Book 1 (18110) LE
  Book 2 (18111) EI
  Book 3 (18112) I–LI
Mr. A. Presents . . .
  First Lyric Pieces (14768) LE
  First Ragtime Pieces (16875) LE
  First Showstoppers! (14769) LE

Performing in Style (412) I
Planet Earth (6022) LI–EA
Sacred Silhouettes (6001) LI
Sacred Silhouettes Revisited (11752) EI–LI
Showstoppers! (11729) I–LI
Simply Sensational!
  Book 1 (6040) LE
  Book 2 (6041) EI
Simply Sonatinas
  Book 1 (6511) LE–EI
  Book 2 (6520) I–LI
Splash of Color, A
  Book 1 (268) EI
  Book 2 (269) I
24 Character Preludes
  Book & CD (20752) LI–EA
  Book (17214)
With These Hands (18555) EA
  CD (18543)

SOLO SHEETS

Early Elementary
  Black Cats Waltzing (18190)
  Happy Halloween Night (3615)
Elementary
  Caterpillar Blues (18151)
  Dolly the Dolphin (18764)
  Gold Medal March (24185)
  It's a Scary Night! (3614)
  Magic of Clouds, The (22398)
  March King (19758)
  My Favorite Kinds of Things (5403)
  Near the Cross (18885)
  Old Daddy Long Legs (20745)
  Traffic Zoo! (14290)
  Very Happy Song, A (22458)
  Who's That Knockin'? (17591)
Late Elementary
  Angry Alligator, The (21315)
  Apache Braves (19682)
  Blackbeard's Bounty (25922)
  Happy Halloween Machine (14231)
  Hazy, Lazy Days (20755)
  Lost Troubador, The (19733)
  Pranksters (3673)
  Pumpkin Boogie (3613)
  Shelby's Great Adventure (26287)
  Shout It Out! (18133)
  Silly Nilly Waltz (19703)
  Springboard (5460)
  Three Bears a-Walkin' (14261)
  Three-Legged Witch, The (3612)
  Touch a Rainbow (3676)
  Tough Cookie! (3638)
  Valse Semplice (5407)
  Willy-Nilly March (3637)
  Wonderful Day!, A (25472)

Early Intermediate
  Buffoons (5473)
  Busybody (29134)
  Close Caper! (5410)
  Ghost of Halloween Past, The (5454)
  Glacier Majesty (5463)
  March of the Great Pumpkins (5453)
  Poco Locomotion (19775)
  Toccata Vivo (18171)
  Valse Romantique (18877)
Intermediate
  Adiós, el Amor Dulce (22494)
  Chanson Triste (5300)
  Christmas Angels, The (Recital Suite) (22416)
  Dizzy Delight (18538)
  Dreamin' (3636)
  El Zapateado (21337)
  Elegy (for left hand alone) (5485)
  Gardens in the Mist (17598)
  Mooncrossing (5491)
  My Faith Looks Up to Thee (14249)
  Newport Rock (18149)
  Notturno (14704)
  Prelude and Toccata (22535)
  Preludium and Toccata
    (for five-octave synthesizer) (11746)
  Rhythm Roulette (24474)
  Souvenir (5387)
  Toccata Brillante (5308)
  Trees Whisper (19754)
  Turboccata (14209)
  Valse élégante (27601)
  Valse Moderne (20735)
Late Intermediate
  Be Still My Soul (18879)
  Danse Humoresque (5458)
  Everlasting (28191)
  Great Northwest, The (Recital Suite) (23248)
  Kansas (Recital Suite) (29167)
  O Little Town of Bethlehem (14289)
  Peaceful Hearts
    (for right hand alone) (18995)
  Reverie in F Minor (18987)
  Serenade in E-flat Major (3670)
  Tarantella Burleska (3674)
  Toccata Spirito (5406)
Early Advanced
  Arioso (for right hand alone) (14291)
  Journey of the Heart (20751)

Simply Classic Series
  Liszt/Hungarian Rhapsody No. 2 (14339)
  Martini/Plaisir D'Amour (14340)
  Rossini/William Tell Overture (14342)
  Schubert/March Militaire (Theme) (14343)

Correlating with
Alfred's Basic Piano Library
Level 3
  Always You (2609)
  Bourrée in D Minor (2611)
  Bridge over Nishigawa (2610)
Level 4
  Mazurka (2612)
  Tender Moments (2614)
  Topsy Turvy Rag (2613)

DUET COLLECTIONS

Five-Star Classical Duets (21347) LE
Five-Star Christmas Duets (23233) E–LE
Five-Star Folk Duets (19792) E
Five-Star Patriotic Duets (20776) LE
Five-Star Sacred Duets (21348) LE
Folk Song Portraits (364) EI
Jazz SophistiCAT (Alexander/Thurmond)
  Duet Book 1 (14717) LE–EI
  Duet Book 2 (14718) I
  GM Disk 1 (14408)
  GM Disk 2 (14409)
Just for You and Me
  Book 1 (6657) LE–EI
  Book 2 (6658) EI–LI
Magic of Christmas, The
  Book 1 (653) EI–I
  Book 2 (235) EI
Sacred Portraits (6003) I
'Twas the Night Before . . . (6683) LE

DUET, DUO AND TRIO SHEETS

Early Elementary
  Holly and the Ivy, The (1p, 6h) (14235)
  March in Cyberspace (1p, 4h) (18152)
  Wild Horse Round-Up (1p, 4h) (22514)
Early Intermediate
  Preludium in D Major (1p, 4h) (3626)
  Star Gazing (1p, 4h) (5449)
Intermediate
  Coventry Carol, The (1p, 4h) (8425)
  Festival in Córdoba (1p, 4h) (3625)
  Festival Overture (1p, 4h) (5411)
  Flirtatious! (2p, 4h) (18161)
  Valse Caprice (1p, 4h) (5441)
Late Intermediate
  Fanfare Toccata-Rondo (2p, 4h) (20778)
Early Advanced
  God Rest Ye Merry, Gentlemen
    (1p, 4h) (18979)

CONCERTOS (2p, 4h)

Concertino in D Major (11769) LI
  GM Disk (14669)
Concertante in G Major (18103) EA

Educational Leveling Chart

EE . . . . . . Early Elementary
E . . . . Elementary
LE . . . . . . Late Elementary
EI . . . . Early Intermediate
I . . . . Intermediate
LI . . . . Late Intermediate
EA . . . . . . Early Advanced
A . . . . Advanced

UK Exam Grade Chart

LE . . . . . . UK Exam Grade 1
EI . . . . . . UK Exam Grade 2
I . . . . UK Exam Grades 3–4
LI . . . . . . UK Exam Grades 4–5
EA . . . . . UK Exam Grades 6–7
A . . . . UK Exam Grades 7–8

ISBN-10: 0-7390-7359-1
ISBN-13: 978-0-7390-7359-9

36348 Book   US $7.99

0 38081 40280 2

alfred.com

50799

9 780739 073599

book two

learn
to play
the
french horn!

A CAREFULLY GRADED METHOD THAT DEVELOPS WELL-ROUNDED MUSICIANSHIP **BY WILLIAM EISENHAUER**

Alfred